How Do You Haiku?

A Step-by-Step Guide with Templates

How Do You Haiku?

By

Danna Smith

Plumbago Press / Woodbridge, CA

Plumbago Press
P.O. Box 101
Woodbridge, CA 95258

www.plumbagopress.com

How Do You Haiku?: A Step-by-Step Guide with Templates by Danna Smith -1st ed

ISBN 979-8-9887378-0-3 Hardcover

ISBN 979-8-9887378-1-0 Paperback

ISBN 979-8-9887378-2-7 E-book

Library of Congress Control Number: 2023914482

Contents

small forgotten seed
of a poem sprouts inside me,
lifting its green head

—Kate Coombs

Introduction

A poet is a special kind of person. One can arrange ordinary letters of the alphabet in powerful ways to move a reader to feel happy, sad, or thoughtful. A poet feels things deeply. They have an active imagination and look at things in unique ways. While one person may see a weeping willow tree, a poet may see the wrinkly face of an old man in the rough gray bark. Another may see hair braids in the branches blowing wildly in the wind.

There are many ways to write a poem, but haiku, the poetry we explore in this book, is the world's most popular form. Haiku encourages you to slow down, go outside, and write about what you see—to capture one moment in time. It is brief yet beautiful and helps us to look at the world differently.

You may be wondering if you can be a haiku writer. The answer is a thousand times YES! Japanese poet Matsuo Basho (1644-1694) said, "If you write five haiku in a lifetime, you are a haiku writer. If you write ten, you are a master." What he was saying is that it's important to practice. The more poems you write, the better poet you'll be. Follow the simple steps in this book to learn how to write haiku and have fun with crafty ways to share your poetry with your friends and family.

This is Matsuo Basho's most famous haiku:

old pond-
frog jumps in
sound of water

The rules for traditional Japanese haiku run deep and can get complicated, but in this book, we will focus on haiku in its simplest form. So, are you ready to get started? Great, like the frog in Basho's poem, let's jump into haiku and make a splash!

What is Haiku?

Haiku (hi-koo), means "light verse." It is a spin-off of a poetry form called Hokku and one of the oldest forms of poetry in the world.

At its center, haiku are unrhymed three-line poems that focus on nature and are written in simple language. The plural of haiku is haiku (no "s").

In the traditional Japanese form, haiku has 17 syllables arranged in a pattern of 5/7/5. That's five syllables in the first line, seven in the second line, and five in the last line.

Haiku started as a party game in Japan over 700 years ago. Friends gathered in a group and took turns writing a two or three-line poem that they would then link together for a long group poem called *haikai no renga (known today as renga).*

To make a good opening for the renga, the host or a party guest would write a three-line poem to get the group started. These three starting lines were called *hokku* (hoe'k-coo).

The hokku was not meant to stand on its own, only to be a part of a sequence of poems. Two hundred years ago, all that changed when a poet named Masaoka Shiki took the three lines of the *hokku,* called them *haiku,* and created a stand-alone poem that an individual, rather than a group, could write.

Haiku is about one moment in time —an ant teetering on a blade of grass, the smell of a sudden rain shower, or the beat of a hummingbird's wings. A moment so small that if you blink, you might miss it. Capturing these moments with words is haiku.

**hit by
a raindrop—
a snail closes up**

—Yosa Buson

In the late 19th century, haiku was introduced to America, Europe, Australia, and other regions. Poets embraced the Japanese tradition, and writing haiku spread like wildflowers!

A Note on Translation

Early Japanese poets originally wrote their haiku in Japanese. Luckily, many haiku have been translated into English for us to enjoy. Words in English and Japanese don't have the same number of syllables; therefore, translators must capture what the poem is about while using words to match the English syllable count. Basho's famous frog poem has been translated hundreds of times by different poets. Here, you will find Basho's original frog poem written in Japanese, followed by several translations. Each is a bit different, but the main feeling of Basho's haiku remains:

古池や　蛙飛び込む　水の音

fura ike ya
kawazu tobikomu
mizu no oto

　　　　　—Matsuo Basho, Japanese poet

**the old pond
a frog jumps in,
water's sound**

—Basho (trans. Ueda)

**At the ancient pond,
a frog takes a sudden plunge
The sound of water**

—Basho (trans. S.A Carter)

**The old pond
The sound
of a frog jumping into the water**

—Basho (trans. Blyth)

Millions of people around the world write and read haiku every day. Why is haiku so popular? Maybe writers like the challenge of "painting" a brief yet vivid word picture. Perhaps they see glimmers of hope in the small, simple things around them, or maybe writing and reading haiku helps them relax. You may have heard the expression, "Big things come in small packages." Haiku is a way for a writer to express big feelings in little winking views of a moment.

1 2 3
0 5 8 4
9 7 10 6

Counting Syllables

You know haiku sometimes has seventeen syllables, but what is a syllable? A syllable is a unit of speech sound. All words have them. Syllables give your poetry a steady rhythm. Here are two ways to help you count syllables:

Clapping

Put your hands together and clap each time you hear a vowel sound. Try it with the following words:

Blue: One clap = one syllable (**blue**).

Thunder: Two claps = two syllables (**thun-der**)

Poetry: Three claps = three syllables (**po-et-ry**).

Chin Movement

Put your hand under your chin and count how many times it moves. Here are a few words to try:

Moon: Chin moves once = one syllable (**moon**).

Haiku: Chin moves two times = two syllables (**hai-ku).**

Dragonfly: Chin moves three times = three syllables (**dra-gon-fly).**

Senryu, Haiku's Cousin

Traditionally, Japanese haiku had strict rules requiring them to be about nature and seasons. With modern haiku, that rule still applies.

But wait, you say you've read haiku that wasn't about nature or seasons?—this is where things get a bit tricky! Haiku has a close cousin named Senryu (*sen-you-rue*), and, like twins, they can be hard to tell apart. Here's an easy way to tell the difference between the two:

- **Haiku** is all about **NATURE.** It can be thoughtful, sad, or funny, but nature and seasons are **always** at the center of the poem (what the poem is mostly about).

- **Senryu** is about **HUMAN NATURE**. It focuses on people, emotions, and behavior. It is humorous and often pokes fun at a situation. Although it sometimes has elements of nature or animals, nature isn't at the poem's center.

Read the following two poems and see if you can tell which poem is haiku and which is senryu:

tiny sentences
brushing soft on my shutters
bush-clover voices

> —Sesshi

chocolate ice cream race,
my hungry puppy and me—
who can lick faster?

> —Danna Smith

You are correct if you guessed the first poem is haiku, and the second is senryu. Sesshi's haiku focuses on nature and has a season word (kigo). We'll learn more about kigo in the following chapters. Sesshi wrote about the bush clover scratching at his window shutters. Bush clover is a sign of autumn in Japan.

The senryu looks like a haiku but isn't about nature. It's about the relationship between a child and a pet (human nature).

Below are two "Catku" by Lee Wardlaw. With these two look-a-like poems, it is even harder to distinguish haiku from senryu! Can you guess which poem is which?

feline in distress
evil couch caught catnip mouse!
you to the rescue

    —Lee Wardlaw

Plump mouse crouched between
two damp leaves. sun-warmed sandwich,
whisker lickin good

    —Lee Wardlaw

You're correct if you guessed the first poem is senryu, and the second is haiku. Both are three-line poems that follow a 5/7/5 syllable count, and while they are both humorous, the haiku places a cat in a garden among leaves and sunshine, and the senryu "paints" an image of the inside of a house and contains human emotion (the cat is worried, and someone helps)

Here are three poems that link together to make one poem. All three verses are written in a three-line format, but clearly, this is senryu, not haiku, because it is titled (haiku is never titled), and the focus is on human nature (a volcano science project and the emotions behind it):

Science Project

O, Dormant Cone, fear
not! I am Pélé, Goddess
of Fire, who rules your

throat and ire. Awake!
Swallow my potion! Release
what smolder, sickens,

below. You choke. Cough.
Burble scarlet froth! My class
erupts in applause.

> —Lee Wardlaw

Now you know how to tell these tricky cousins apart. If you see a haiku that isn't about nature, it is probably really a senryu. Both forms are fun to write!

In the next chapter, you will find a checklist of simple points to help you write your best haiku ever!

Haiku Checklist

What Your Haiku Really Wants

- #1 Three short lines
- #2 Imagery
- #3 The real deal
- #4 Season words
- #5 Feeling
- #6 Love of nature
- #7 "Ah!" moment

#1 THREE SHORT LINES

There are two ways of writing modern haiku; both feature three lines. One way is writing haiku in a 5-7-5 pattern of counted syllables. That's 5 syllables in the first line, 7 in the second line, and 5 in the third line for a total of 17 syllables. Here are examples of this kind of haiku:

deep within the ground (5)
snuggled inside a small hole (7)
tiny eyes open (5)

> —Linda Whalen

if you are butter (5)
I'm cup, fluttering yellow (7)
meadows of laughter (5)

> —Raven Howell

tiny living lights (5)
twinkle in summer night skies (7)
have you seen fireflies? (5)

> —Bobi Martin

Traditional Japanese haiku follows a pattern of 5-7-5 sounds. These sounds are not syllables but sounds called "on" (pronounced "own"). An important thing to note is that Japanese sound counts differ from English syllable counts. So, if you write a 5-7-5 poem in English, you are writing a longer poem than a 5-7-5 Japanese poem. Sometimes, this longer poem can feel "clunky" or be hard to read, so some poets prefer to write three brief lines without counting syllables.

Do this: take a breath in and then let it out. That didn't take long, did it? That is how brief the haiku is—just one breath long. It's also as long as it takes for a frog to jump into the water or a flower petal to fall to the ground. The following examples are haiku written in three brief lines without a specific syllable count:

frost-stung (2)
morning awakens (5)
ice and earnest souls (5)
   —Matt Forrest Esenwine

a frog floating (4)
in the water jar (4)
rain of summer (4)
   —Masaoka Shiki

Somersaulting (4)
    on a searing breeze (5)
        yellow swallowtail (5)

—Amy Losak with Syd Rosenberg

So, which is the correct way to write modern haiku? Both styles are acceptable! Every poet has a preference. Do you like the "word puzzle" of counting syllables, or do you want to write three brief lines no longer than a breath? You are the boss of your haiku!

A Note About Line Structure

There are several styles of line structure in haiku. All the examples below are acceptable. It's the poet's choice! The most popular method (and the structure of Linda Hoffman Kimball's original poem below) is to line up your lines to the left:

mallards on the lake
seem to scatter emeralds
when they shake their heads

—Linda Hoffman Kimball

Some poets indent their lines "step style":

mallards on the lake
> **seem to scatter emeralds**
>> **when they shake their heads**

Centering the haiku is another popular choice:

mallards on the lake
seem to scatter emeralds
when they shake their heads

There is also a single horizontal line structure with spaces between groups of words. This structure works well with short haiku:

caught   a firefly   in the mind's darkness

—Yosa Buson

#2 IMAGERY

"Painting" an image with words is essential for writing a good haiku. Imagery is a word or group of words that tap into the senses. Writing about what you can smell, hear, taste, see, or touch in nature will create strong images in your haiku.

In the haiku below, Raven Howell has created a poem that bursts with imagery. Can you "see" the image she has sketched? Would you have stopped what you were doing to write about this passing moment?

sun plays hide and seek
suddenly clouds spill out rain
watercolor spring

—Raven Howell

To "sketch" an image, your words need to be descriptive. For example, instead of saying "a tree," you could say "frosty aspens glisten." Or, instead of saying "a flower," you could say "wilted daisy in the sunshine."

These examples use a "trick" that connects the main image to something else to show a relationship between the two images:

aspen + frost = glisten

daisy + sunshine = wilt

moon + water = shimmer.

You don't have "glisten," "wilt," or "shimmer" without the two images together.

Here is an example of Boncho's poem (translated as four lines) using this trick (silent + topple = echo):

**in silent mid-night
our old scarecrow
topples down
weird hollow echo**

—Nozawa Boncho

Using **sensory words** is a great way to create imagery in your poems. You may **hear** a woodpecker *tap-tap* on an oak tree nearby or **smell** a musty summer lake. Perhaps you **taste** a sweet, juicy peach picked fresh off the branch. Pay attention to what you hear, smell, taste, see, or feel, and use it in your haiku.

#3 THE REAL DEAL

While riding your bike, you feel the crisp wind on your skin, smell freshly mowed grass on a summer night, or look down and see a dandelion growing in the sidewalk's crack. These are haiku moments. When we slow down and look at the world around us, we can appreciate the small things happening at that moment.

Sometimes, what you see will make you feel sad:

cemetery gate
black ants march toward headstone
visiting grandma

> —Danna Smith

Sometimes haiku moments make you laugh:

In my small village
    even the flies
    aren't afraid
to bite a big man

> —Issa (trans. P. Beilenson, Behn)

Haiku can also help you feel calm:

the cornstalks whisper
their deep secrets to the wind
knowing they're kept safe

> —Linda Hoffman Kimball

Haiku is happening all around us—all the time. The trick is to pay attention and think deeply about what we see. When writing haiku, try to write from actual experiences. What you witness first-hand will give you details you wouldn't have had if you had written from your imagination.

An excellent example of writing from a real experience comes from haiku master Basho and another of his famous poems. Basho was a poetry teacher who lived simply. His students planted a banana tree (a *basho* tree) beside his hut. In 1681, he wrote this poem about the banana tree as he worried that the rapidly growing reed grass (ogi) would take the nutrients his tree would need to grow:

**we planted the banana tree
and now I hate the first sprouts
of the ogi reeds**

—Matsuo Basho

Remember, haiku doesn't have to be serious all the time. Humorous moments are happening in nature right now! If you see something funny, write about it.

a warbler
poops
on a slender plum branch

—Uejima Onitsura

I toss in my sleep,
so watch out,
cricket!

—Kobayashi Issa (trans. Michael R. Burch)

4 SEASON WORDS

Haiku is all about seasons, but the poet rarely mentions the season directly. Instead, they replace the words winter, spring, summer, and fall with *kigo* (a season word). For example, when we read about tulips, we know it is springtime without reading the word "spring." Likewise, when we read a poem about crisp brown maple leaves, we know it is autumn. Kigo acts like a "hint" for the reader.

American poet Nancy Etchemendy used the kigo *apricots* in the haiku below. She didn't tell the reader it is summer, but we know because that's when apricots ripen on the trees.

gold moons in a tree
the apricots have ripened
each one a sweet kiss

—Nancy Etchemendy

Here's another example. This haiku is from Japanese poet Matsuo Basho. The kigo is cherry trees:

under cherry trees
soup, the salad, fish and all
seasoned with petals
     —Matsuo Basho

We know it is springtime in this haiku because spring is when cherry trees blossom. Close your eyes. Can you "see" Basho's picnic sprinkled with fragrant pink petals?

Of course, poets sometimes choose not to use kigo in their haiku (remember, they are the boss of their haiku). Below is an example of this kind of haiku. Japanese poet Issa uses the actual season name here (autumn):

yellow autumn moon
unimpressed the scarecrow stands
simply looking bored
     —Kobayashi Issa

Why do you think Issa used the season's name in his haiku? We can only guess. Perhaps he used the word autumn because the season of the poem isn't clear without it. Scarecrows keep watch over fields in autumn, but you can also see scarecrows in

30

spring, summer, and winter. Using both words (scarecrow and autumn) has made the season clear and painted a vivid fall picture.

Japanese haiku poets collect season words in a season word dictionary called a *saijiki* (sah-ee-jee-key). This handy dictionary lists thousands of seasonal words that help a poet write vivid haiku. Each season breaks down into seven groups or themes:

Weather:
The climate, months, length of day, temperature.

The heavens:
Sky, space, wind, storms, light, shade.

Earth:
Seascapes, fields, forests, meadows, lakes, mountains.

Humanity:
Clothes, food, sports, work, play.

Holidays:
National holidays and celebrations.

Animals:
Mammals, reptiles, birds, fish, insects.

Plants:
Blossoming trees, flowers, ripe vegetables and fruit, seaweed, fungi.

For example, if you live in northern California in the United States, your summer kigo might look something like this:

Weather: sweltering heat, muggy, scorching, humid.

The Heavens: blue sky, hot air balloon, strawberry moon.

The Earth: ocean, orchard, mountains, vineyard, breeze.

Humanity: run in sprinklers, swim, cold drinks, sunglasses.

Holidays: Fourth of July, Father's Day, Labor Day.

Animals: mosquitos, snails, house flies, bumble bees.

Plants: blackberry, sunflower, weeds, strawberries.

Your summer kigo will be quite different if you live in Japan:

Summer Weather: hot, cool night, short night.

The Heavens: cloudy, summer moon, rainy, thunder.

The Earth: waterfall, clear water, green paddy (rice field).

Humanity: summer kimono, new tea, straw mats.

Holidays: Lunar Summer's End, Boy's Day (tango).

Animals: sweet fish, kingfisher, moth, cicada.

Plants: leafing cherry, shade of trees, bamboo shoots.

As you can see, kigo helps haiku poets create detailed images that make their haiku shine!

Later in this book, you will have an opportunity to create your own mini saijiki that you can turn to when writing your haiku.

#5 FEELING

Haiku can make you feel emotions like loneliness, grief, fear, or joy. The feeling is never said directly. Instead, the emotion is "shown" through the image the poet paints with words. Instead of saying "the sad dog," you could say, "lost puppy in a storm." With these descriptive words, your reader can imagine the dog is cold, hungry, afraid, and, therefore, sad.

Haiku wins when we can connect a subject to a deep feeling. In this haiku, poets Amy Losak and Sydell Rosenberg "show" readers that the subject (a yellow iris) is confident without saying it outright.

**like a lion queen
a large yellow iris roars
"I rule this garden!"**
—Amy Losak with Sydell Rosenberg

In the following poem, Issa could have said, "The spiders are afraid," but he told a story with his words to paint an image that "shows" readers the spiders might be worried about being swept away with the dust:

34

don't worry, spiders
I keep house
casually

—Kobayashi Issa (trans. Robert Hass)

Japanese Cutting Words

In Japanese haiku, a kiregi (key-ray-jee) is a cutting word. Cutting words create a pause or a break between parts of the poem. They give haiku more meaning and feeling by creating contrast or surprise. The Japanese language has a special group of words they use as cutting words. In Basho's original famous frog poem below, "ya" is a cutting word. It gives the reader a clue as to how to read the poem:

Furu ike ya
Kawazu tobikomu
Mizy no oto

In translating the poem to English, the translator uses a dash in place of the cutting word "ya":

The old pond—
A frog leaps in
And a splash

—Matsuo Basho (trans. Ueda)

35

In the following translation to English, an ellipsis is used to convey the pause that the cutting word created. In both examples, we are forced to hesitate after the word "pond:"

an old pond...
a frog leaps in,
sound of water

—Basho (trans. Shirane)

English does not have a category of cutting words, so we use punctuation like ellipses, commas, dashes, or exclamation points. Periods should never be used at the end of lines in a haiku and are used sparingly in the middle of a line.

Here's an example of using punctuation as cutting words. Angie Quantrell creates pauses (exclamation points) and surprise (a dash) in her linked poem about a fairy house built on a sandy beach and then damaged by a storm. This poem is also an excellent example of humor in haiku:

summer fairy house
make believe play at the beach
move in ready pad

crash! whoosh! boom! a storm
thunders through, rearranges—
fixer upper sale

—Angie Quantrell

Don't worry too much about the placement of your punctuation at first. Try to get the "image" down on paper. Then, you can return to your poem and insert the punctuation needed.

#6 LOVE OF NATURE

Haiku is a brief poem filled with compassion for nature. There is no room for hatred, violence, or cruelty. Basho said, "Every form of insentient existence—plants, stones, or utensils—has its individual feelings similar to those of men."

Basho's dragonfly story is an excellent example of having a loving attitude toward nature and its creatures.

One day, a student named Takarai Kikaku and Basho were walking and spotted dragonflies buzzing among the flowers. Kikaku thought the body of the red dragonfly looked like a pepper pod. He wrote this haiku and showed it to Basho:

a red dragonfly!
remove its wings—
a pepperpod!

Basho said, "The dragonfly is dead." He then drafted a poem showing compassion toward the dragonfly, saying, "This is how to create life."

red pepperpods
add wings—
behold dragonflies!

#7 "AH!" MOMENT

Your haiku should end in a way that surprises or enlightens your reader. The surprise makes us say, "Ah! I understand," "Ah! That's funny," or "Ah! So true!" The surprise comes at the end of the haiku. It's more of a "quiet-friendly-smile-surprise" than a "jump-out-of-a-dark-room" surprise. It's a subtle (not shocking) turn or change in the poem.

> **in the thick green veins**
> **of a crimson maple leaf**
> **a million trees roar**
>
> —Amy Losak with Syd Rosenberg

When you read the last line of this haiku, were you surprised? Did you expect the poem's meaning to switch to the family history or DNA of the leaf? As readers, we might not predict what happens next, but the surprise gives our hearts a little lift, a stab of sadness, or helps us see something with understanding and fresh eyes.

Haiku in Review

What You've Learned

The following chapter will guide you through writing your first haiku. Let's review what you've learned so far:

- Haiku is kind.
- Haiku is about nature and seasons.
- Haiku is three short lines (syllable count or not).
- Descriptive words help readers "see" the image.
- Haiku can be sad, thoughtful, or funny.
- Haiku is from real experiences.
- Haiku is written in the present tense (here and now).
- Haiku does not rhyme.
- Haiku is not titled.
- Capitalization isn't used in modern haiku (except for "I").
- Punctuation (Kireji) is used to create a pause.
- Haiku ends with a surprise or an "ah!" moment.

Read Haiku

The Best Way to Understand

Matsuo Basho said, "Learn about the pine from the pine and the bamboo from the bamboo." Meaning that you should learn about something from the thing itself. One of the best ways to understand how to write haiku is to read haiku.

There is a library list of favorite books containing haiku in the back pages of this handbook. But for now, you can read the following traditional Japanese haiku and modern haiku from current poets.

Take your time, pause, and reflect on the images that the poems create in your mind. Ask yourself these questions: What season is it in each poem? Is there a season word? What emotion do I feel after reading this poem? Which is my favorite poem and why?

winter blizzard
I donate a carrot nose
for the snowman's face

—Sydell Rosenberg

buzzing the bee trades
peony for peony
with the butterfly

—Taigi (trans. P. Beilenson)

spring rain
the frog's bellies
aren't yet wet

—Yosa Buson

a baby crab
climbs up my leg
such clear water

—Matsuo Basho

across nature trail
shafts of sunlight sketch
hopscotch for squirrels

—Danna Smith

snow melting...
the village is flooded
with children

—Kobayashi Issa

this man who seems cruel,
throws bits of bread to sparrows
I have found him out

—Nancy Etchemendy

while a cicada
sings softly
a single leaf falls ...

—Kobayashi Issa (trans. R. Burch)

a short summer night
the hairy caterpillar wears
pearls of dew

—Yosa Buson

harvest moon sketches
crane on ceiling
at midnight
—Danna Smith

plump bumble bees
play tag in the hollyhocks—
pollen on their knees

—Linda Hoffman Kimball

clouds passing over—
a dog peeing on the run,
village winter shower

—Matsuo Basho

distant mountains
reflected in the eye
of a dragonfly

—Kobayashi Issa

new snow lies lovely
out front. But in the garage
the snow shovel sighs

—Kate Coombs

summer shower
beats the heads
of carp

—Masaoka Shiki

holding umbrellas
children, like rows of mushrooms
glisten in the rain

—Sydell Rosenberg

geodes hide magic!
break one open and see
an amazing surprise!

—Bobi Martin

two maple leaves swirl
overlapping as they land
a tent for a mouse

—Linda Hoffman Kimball

Writing Your First Haiku

Practice Makes Progress

Now that you've learned the rules of haiku and read examples, it's time to write your first haiku!

This chapter will guide you step-by-step through finding images, selecting the best words, and showing you easy formulas to create your poems. Level up as your skills develop.

Level 1— Simplified Haiku

At this level, we concentrate on the "where," "what," and "when" of the haiku moment without a specific syllable count, as in this example:

Where it happens:	on grandma's porch
What is happening:	beetle on its back
When it happens:	stormy morning

Step 1: Look outside and select an object from nature.

butterfly

Step 2: Make a list of descriptive phrases that tell **where** the haiku moment is happening.

on a green leaf
in the park
on my brother's hand
among wildflowers
on a pink rose petal

Step 3: Create a list of descriptive phrases describing **what** is happening.

hungry butterfly sips nectar
tiny butterfly feet tickle
butterfly flaps colorful wings
butterfly makes a friend
butterflies dance

Step 4: Brainstorm a list of phrases that tell **when** the haiku moment is happening.

> **at dawn**
> **one summer day**
> **at lunchtime**
> **one hot afternoon**
> **all day long**

Step 5: Choose a "**where**," "**what**" and "**when**" phrase from each list and write your haiku in three lines. You can adjust the wording as needed. These brainstorming sessions are a great way to help you with ideas but shouldn't restrict you.

(where)	**among wildflowers** (6)
(what)	**butterflies dance** (4)
(when)	**at dawn** (2)

You have written your first haiku! If you'd like, you can swap the "where" and "what" lines:

(what)	**butterflies dance** (4)
(where)	**among wildflowers** (6)
(when)	**at dawn** (2)

LEVEL 2— TRADITIONAL HAIKU

At this level, you will be guided through five interactive steps to create a traditional 17-syllable haiku. Let's get started!

Step 1: Go outside and select an object from nature.

dandelion

Step 2: Use as many of the five senses as possible to create a list of words and phrases describing the object. What does it look like? Touch it—what does it feel like? How does it smell? Does it make a sound? How does the object make you feel? What do you think the object might be feeling?

summertime
springtime
bees love them
they love bees
soft petals
short green stem
fluffy seed ball
prickly leaves
not fragrant
blowing white fluff
covering the lawn
going to seed
making a wish
hopeful
close up at night
happy yellow flowers

Step 3: Brainstorm a haiku idea by creating sentences using the ideas from Step 2. Write down anything that comes to your mind.

Bumble bees love the pretty yellow flowers.
Blowing white fluff makes me happy.
Fluffy seed balls spread hope.
Bright flowers cover the lawn like yellow polka dots.
How many wishes in one puff?

Step 4: Write a haiku with ideas from your sentences. Don't worry about the syllable count for now.

fluffy seed ball (4)
ready, set, blow (4)
dandelion summer (6)

Step 5: Rewrite and adjust the wording to create a 17-syllable haiku with 5 syllables in the first line, 7 in the second line, and 5 in the third line. Notice the changes made to the haiku above to create the correct syllable count for the revised haiku below.

white fluffy seed ball, (5)
wishes blowing in the wind—(7)
dandelion spring (5)

Editing Your Haiku

Making it Shine

There is a saying, "A great story (or poem) isn't written; it's rewritten." That means once you have written your haiku, it's time to read it aloud and clean it up with small changes to make it shine!

Omit

Get rid of lazy words like an, a, the, and is. Lazy words don't give your readers a specific image in their minds. Use descriptive words instead (not "a tree" but "bare tree" or "aspen tree.").

Check

Check that your poem has a little surprise at the end (an "ah" moment). Also, check that you didn't give your haiku a title. If you can't understand the poem without a title, try to work the main topic into the poem's text.

Scan

Scan your poem for capitalizations and periods. Remember, haiku is not a sentence (it's art!), so we don't usually use periods at the end of lines or capitalization in modern haiku (except for the word "I"). Use "I" and "me" sparingly. Haiku is not about you but about little moments in nature happening around you.

Count

If you wrote your poem with a syllable count, check if it follows the 5-7-5 pattern.

Now, let's put those haiku skills to work! The following chapters contain tips to help you write your first haiku and will introduce you to fun and creative haiku activities for you and your friends to try.

Create a Saijiki

Your Season Word Dictionary

As discussed earlier in the chapter, *Haiku Checklist*, haiku is all about seasons, but the poet rarely mentions the season directly. Instead, they replace the words winter, spring, summer, and fall with *kigo* (season words). Every country or region has its own weather and kigo.

Hundreds of years ago, Japanese poets collected their kigo in a *Saijiki* (Season Word Dictionary). You can create your own Saijiki (sah-ee-jee-key) with the following template that will help guide you as you write haiku. **If this is not your book, please do not write in it. Instead, make copies of the worksheets (one set for each season).** Then, write your kigo on the copy, cut, and staple the pages together. You now have a mini saijiki!

MY SAIJIKI season_____

Heavens:

_____   _____
_____   _____
_____   _____

Earth:

_____   _____
_____   _____
_____   _____

Humanity:

_____   _____
_____   _____
_____   _____

Holidays:

_____   _____
_____   _____
_____   _____

MY SAIJIKI

season_____

Animals:

_____ _____
_____ _____
_____ _____

Plants:

_____ _____
_____ _____
_____ _____

Weather:

_____ _____
_____ _____
_____ _____

Write a Picture Haiku

Visualize Your Poem

A picture haiku is a modern way to visualize your poem. Go outside and snap a picture, rip an image from a magazine, or open the gallery in your phone and choose a picture you've already taken. Study the picture. How do you feel? If the image could talk, what message would it tell you?

For example, in the picture on the next page, it might look like the mailbox is wading into a sea of flowers, maybe there is a surprise inside the mailbox, or perhaps the mailbox ate the mail too fast, and it's going to burrrrp any minute! Take time to study the photo. Use your imagination. Maybe the flowers at the base of the mailbox are waiting for a letter from someone. Who do you think would send that letter?

Keep asking questions until you get an idea for a haiku, then print and tape the picture into your poem journal (we'll explore poetry journals a bit later). Now, write your haiku next to the image. There are endless possibilities hidden inside every photo.

Here's a picture haiku example using the photo above:

poppies by mailbox
awaiting love letter from
wandering violet

—Danna Smith

In this beautiful picture haiku, Angie Quantrell has linked two haiku to make a longer poem called a *rensaku (ray'n-sah-coo)*, a series of haiku linked together to tell a "story." Each haiku makes sense if you read it independently. Here's Angie's *picture haiku rensaku* (say that five times fast!).

Photo by Angie Quantrell ©2021

seeking light, water
face to the sun, wearing your
tiny fairy hat

buds tight with promise
urgency to bloom and seed
hello leek princess
       —Angie Quantrell

Create a Kuhi

Poem Stones

Carving a poem on a stone is an old Asian tradition. These stones, called kuhi (coo-hee), decorate gardens, parks, and temples. There are Japanese gardens worldwide, many of them with poem stones. There are two kuhi gardens in America, one in Seattle, Washington, and the other in Hayward, California.

Why not create your own Kuhi garden? Go outside and find a smooth, flat stone. Paint your rock a base color or add doddles to it. Write your haiku on the stone with a permanent marker or paint pen. When the ink and paint are dry, spray your rocks with clear sealing varnish to protect them from the weather. Make several kuhi to scatter around your yard or give one to a friend.

old pond—
frog jumps in
sound of water

Write a Haibun

Haiku with Story

A Haibun (hi-boon) is a short story with haiku. In Japanese, *hai* means "haiku," and **bun** means "prose" (story or writing). As you know, haiku is a "snapshot" of a moment in time, but mixing poetry and story gives the reader more information to understand the poem better. Japanese poet Matsuo Basho made this form famous during his lifetime in the 1600s.

    Think of a short story and write it down. It could be something fun you did with your friends, a memory from a vacation, or you can capture words from your favorite book. Next, write a haiku on the same page as your story. The haiku doesn't repeat what we've learned from the story; it adds to or completes it.

Remember to use descriptive language. For example, instead of saying "flower garden," you might say "daffodil meadow," or instead of saying "spider web," you might say "silver threads in the moonlight."

Here's a haibun example taken from a childhood memory:

I wanted to plant a garden as a child but had no seeds. So, I improvised. I stuck popsicle sticks into fruit from the kitchen and "planted" beautiful rows of apples and oranges in the soil. My parents were unhappy with me when they returned home to find our fruit in the dirt.

in child's garden,
bright imagination yields
fruitful harvest

       —Danna Smith

This example is from a brightly illustrated handbook on western bluebirds. As you can see, the story that accompanies your haiku in a haibun can vary:

Bluebirds' favorite foods include grasshoppers, crickets, ground beetles, and caterpillars. In addition to insects, bluebirds will feed on berries that ripen in summer.

**bluebird hovering,
lunching on sweet berries served
on pokeweed branches**
—Danna Smith

Renga

Group Linked Poetry

Have you ever run a relay race or watched one on TV? In a relay race, four runners run one race by taking turns. One runner starts the race, and when that runner stops, another steps in, and so on, until all runners have had a chance to run, and the race is complete. Renga is like a relay race. The good news is that the group can be as large as you'd like in renga, and breaking a sweat is not required.

As discussed earlier, over seven hundred years ago in Japan, friends joined a group circle and took turns writing a two or three-line poem. They would then link the poems together for a long group poem called "haikai no renga" (known today as renga). As a gift to the host, a party guest would start the poem (using the current season), alternating short-long-short lines (this starting poem was called a hokku but is now known as a haiku). The other guests would then take turns writing a poem linked to the verse before it. Then they combined the poems to make one long renga!

Look at this renga. A selection of links, mid-sequence, written in 1355 and translated by Hiroaki Sato in his book *One Hundred Frogs*:

every evening the vines
on spindle trees
scatter their leaves
　　　—Shigekazu

Elun follows Shigekazu's verse:

because we're in winter
the wind is cold
　　　—Elun

Now, it is Gusai's turn to add his poem:

I see ruts of my small cart
on the morning ice
　　　—Gusia

Ietada adds his poem, taking it in another direction:

the two rivers
have come together
　　　—Ietada

We would have known the season was winter even if Elun hadn't told us because of the other poets' seasonal words, such as cold wind and ice, and, if you are familiar with Japan, you might know the spindle tree loses its leaves in winter. Of course, your season words may differ depending on where you live.

It's Your Turn

Gather with your friends in a circle. Choose a "Sabaki" (sah-bah-key) from the group (a leader who will pick a topic and remind writers to use season words in their poems, starting with the current season). The renga will naturally shift away from the main topic as it grows, and the seasons will change until all seasons are explored. Most renga is 36 to 100 poems long. Your renga can be any length. Keep going around the circle until you are ready to stop. Before you start, you might want to decide as a group how long your renga will be. Don't worry about making your poems perfect. The point is to have fun creating with your friends.

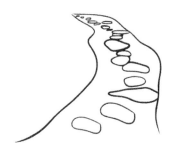

Take a Ginko Walk

Finding a Haiku Moment

A ginko is a quiet walk in nature where you write about what you see. Grab your notebook and head outside. What small moments can you find? What do you feel, see, smell, taste, or hear? Perhaps you see a dragonfly in the reeds. Or maybe you feel an oak tree's bumpy, rough bark. Write a haiku about that very moment. Try to take ginko walks often to capture moments of every season where you live. Use descriptive words to make your poems lively. Here's an example:

**webbed blanket of green
growing on a grey boulder
with a napping snail**
—Linda Whalen

The line, "webbed blanket of green," evokes a much better image than if the poet had written "mossy rock." Word choice is key!

In the example below, Kate Coombs paints a calming word picture for her readers (the kigo is "snow"):

fox was here, a bird
a deer. Their tracks speak out
in the quiet snow

    —Kate Coombs

Can you "see" in your mind what the poet saw? Can you feel the hush of a winter morning?

Create a Haiga

A Drawing with Haiku

Often called Zen Art, Haiga (hi-gah) combines haiku and drawings on the same page. One can visualize a haiku in their mind when reading it, but displaying both the poem and art increases the poetic experience. The splash of water, a leaf drifting on the breeze, a bird perched on a fence post. It's a treat for the eyes and ears!

Japanese poets often create haiga in black ink with simple brush strokes. For example, if you were to add a painting to Basho's Frog poem from the beginning of this book, you might draw a simple swirl of water ripples and then write the poem on the same page. The poetry and the image work together to strengthen the other.

Below is a haiga created by Yosa Buson (1716-1784):

**a little cuckoo
across
the hydrangea**

Buson has drawn a simple cuckoo bird and hydrangea flowers, both of which are season words for summer in Japan. His haiku is written in Japanese vertically down the page. As you can see, haiga is simple yet beautiful:

A Little Cuckoo Across the Hydrangea, Yosa Buson

Try Haiga Blot Painting

You can create your haiga any way you'd like, with markers, watercolors, ink, pencil, or cut paper collage. Paint blots are excellent for haiga because the swipe of paint on paper feels like the simple brush strokes that Japanese poets often use. It's a fun activity for the whole family or classroom.

Grab a small piece of paper or an index card, acrylic paint, and a palette knife (if you don't have a palette knife, the edge of a used gift card works great!). Place a nickel or quarter-sized amount of color on the page. Ready, set, swipe!

What picture do you see in your paint blot? Now, turn it sideways and upside down. Do you see anything different? When the paint is dry, outline the image you've found with a black fine-tip marker or pen and write your haiku on the card, or use one of your favorite haiku you've read in this book. Congratulations, you have created a haiga!

In the example above, a swipe of white paint on gray paper looks like a bird. The paint blot was paired with one of Basho's funny haiku:

good for nothing
I just want to sleep,
noisy bird

 —Basho

Travel Haiku

Taking Haiku on the Road

Basho was a traveler. One spring day in 1689, when he was 45 years old, he sold his home outside of Edo (Tokyo), strapped on his straw sandals, and set out on foot for his last long journey. His disciple, Sora, accompanied him through remote parts of Northern Japan. They met new friends and poets along the way. Basho wrote, "Time after time, new sights stir my spirit."

Of course, there were no cameras back then, so it was usual for travelers to record their journeys in diaries. Being a poet, Basho wrote hokku (now called haiku) in his journals. He also wrote stories about what he saw along the way and added a poem at the end (haibun). A good portion of Basho's haiku you read today are from his travels.

Basho's diary was called *Narrow Road to the Deep North* (Oku no Hosomichi) and has been translated into English numerous times over the last 300 years.

The next time you go on vacation, why not take your notebook, and record your travels with poems rather than photographs? Travel journals aren't like regular diaries; they don't go into detail about everything that happens. Instead, the poet writes a haiku or haibun about a strong image seen along the way. Basho understood this as he once asked the question, "Is there any good in saying everything?" In the examples below from the poetry blog PoetryPop, a trip to the California coast resulted in these travel haiku:

sandpiper on shore
playing chicken with waves
hop! you can't catch me

—Danna Smith

early morning walk
I wrap myself in layers
soft blankets of fog

—Danna Smith

sand dollar on beach
pale canvas holds
nature's petal sketch

—Danna Smith

Gunsaku

More Fun Than a Barrel of Monkeys

A collection of poems on the same subject is called gunsaku (goon-sah-koo). The haiku in gunsaku have a common topic. But the poet writes each haiku from a different point of view. The poems don't build on each other like a story (that's called rensaku). If you pluck one haiku from the grouping, it could stand on its own as a single haiku. While haiku isn't usually titled, a title is necessary with gunsaku to convey the theme.

A Basket of Easter Haiku is a gunsaku of four Easter poems. Notice that although the poems are about a holiday, nature or season words still play a part, and each haiku makes sense on its own.

A BASKET OF EASTER HAIKU

sitting on her eggs
fat red hen dozes,
one eye on bunny

blue butterfly finds
colorful eggs nestled deep
among daffodils

sudden spring shower,
rain decorates pastel eggs
dot, dot, polka dot

in wild bramble
mama bird fills nest with eggs
nature's spring basket

—Danna Smith

Animals in nature often gather in groups. Sometimes these groups have unusual (but real) names like "*a leap of leopards*" or "a *murder of crows.*" The following pages will show you how to expand on this concept for a fun twist when writing gunsaku.

It's Your Turn

Write three or more haiku on the same subject. Remember to keep your poems nature-related and include season words and vivid verbs. Here are haiku grouping ideas for you to try:

Animal Groupings

A Litter of Kitten Haiku

A Gaggle of Geese Haiku

A School of Fish Haiku

A Rhumba of Rattlesnake Haiku

A Pandemonium of Parrot Haiku

A Leap of Leopard Haiku

A Swarm of Bee Haiku

A Flock of Bird Haiku

A Murder of Crow Haiku

A Parade of Elephant Haiku

A Quiver of Cobra Haiku

A Scurry of Squirrel Haiku

A Prickle of Porcupine Haiku

Nature Groupings

A Bouquet of Spring Haiku

A Galaxy of Planet Haiku

A Cluster of Star Haiku

A Bucket of Bug Haiku

A Flicker of Lightning Haiku

A Wave of Ocean Haiku

A Forest of Tree Haiku

A Ripple of River Haiku

A Blizzard of Winter Haiku

Poetry On the Go

Recreate a take on the popular magnetic poetry game using simple items around your house.

What you'll need:

- Card stock or heavy paper
- A pen or marker
- Scissors
- A metal breath mint tin

Write down a list of nouns, verbs, and suffixes (ing, ed, ly, ful). Your words should include weather, Earth, humanity, animals, plants, and holidays. You can use words from your season word dictionary if you'd like! Remember to include dashes, ellipses, exclamation points, and commas.

Cut the words and symbols into small strips. Dump the paper strips onto the table face-up and arrange them into haiku.

When you are finished, store the word strips in the mint tin for safekeeping. Take it with you for poetry on the go!

Game Variation

If you have access to a label maker, you can print the words out on strips of label tape and stick them to small magnet strips purchased from a craft store. You can then use the inside of the metal tin lid (or a baking pan) as a magnetic board to arrange your poetry.

Haiku Comics

Comic strips are a fun way to "haiku." Make a copy of the comic strip template on the next page and start creating! You'll find examples below. Use speech bubbles, thought bubbles, and sound words like *swish, pop,* or *splash*. Anything goes—have fun!

Springtime Haiku

from How Do You Haiku? ©Danna Smith

Haiku Friends

from *How Do You Haiku?* ©Danna Smith

Haiku Templates

Photocopy and Write

Use the following illustrated templates to tickle your imagination and display your work!

Each template provides a primary topic and a place to write your three-line haiku. Photocopy them and share them with your friends, family, or classroom.

You might want to add illustrations to the templates. For example, you could add fish, seashells, or a sandcastle to the beach template or a bee or ladybug to the garden haiku template. Let's get creative!

Dogku

_____

_____

_____

Plumbago Press, *How Do You Haiku?* by Danna Smith

82

Catku

Plumbago Press, *How Do You Haiku?* by Danna Smith

Garden Haiku

_____

_____

_____

Plumbago Press, *How Do You Haiku?* by Danna Smith

Horse Haiku

_____

_____

_____

Plumbago Press, *How Do You Haiku?* by Danna Smith

Frog Haiku

_____

_____

_____

Plumbago Press, *How Do You Haiku?* by Danna Smith

Beach Haiku

_____

_____

_____

Plumbago Press, *How Do You Haiku?* by Danna Smith

Haiku Journal

Keeping it Together

Collect your amazing poems in a journal just like the haiku masters. You can glue or tape your painted index cards (haiga) and photos (picture haiku) into the notebook. Divide your notebook into eight sections:

1. Haiku
2. Haiga
3. Haibun
4. Travel haiku
5. Gunsaku
6. Renga
7. Picture Haiku
8. Comic Haiku

Return to your haiku journal often to add new poems.

Sharing Is Caring

Sharing Your Poetry with Others

You have come a long way in understanding haiku. Are you ready to share your poems with friends and family?

For some, sharing a poem can be like ripping open your heart and showing your secret thoughts and feelings to the world. It can be scary. And it's okay if you want to skip the sharing part. But think about it. You've written a poem only you can write because of your unique viewpoints and experiences. Sharing your work can make others happy and affect lives in ways you'll never know. Think of a favorite poem, song, or painting you've seen or heard. Now, think about how good it made you feel. What if the poet, singer, or artist never shared their work with you? You would have never experienced the joy of their gift.

Sometimes, people think their poem is not "good enough" to share. That's not true. What you write and how you express yourself is a part of you, and your poems and feelings matter.

If you are still shy about sharing, you can start by writing your poem on a greeting card, emailing a haiku to a friend, or texting it. Sharing this way might be easier than showing your poetry to someone in person. In time, you will feel more confident and comfortable with sharing. You will find that people will be happy to receive your poetry gift and will likely want you to write more.

Be brave. You are amazing!

Meet the Haiku Masters

The Great Four

Throughout this book, you've read haiku by Japanese poets Basho, Buson, Issa, and Shiki. They are the great four. Each played an important part in the evolution of the haiku we write today. Their creative strength and style differed, yet they all observed calmly and loved nature and others deeply. Basho said, "Make the universe your companion, always bearing in mind the true nature of things—mountains and river, trees and grasses, and humanity—and enjoy the falling blossoms and the scattering leaves." Take a minute to learn about these poets on the following pages.

Matsuo Basho

falling sick on a journey
my dream wanders around
fields of dry grass

—Basho (1644-1694)

Basho (bah-show) was born Matsuo Kinsaku. As a young boy, he became interested in literature and poetry. At age 30, Basho founded a school and was a beloved poetry teacher and mentor. He was a spiritual man. At age 38, Basho began studying Zen and gave up many comforts of life to live simply. He liked traveling on foot and horseback, drafting poems, meeting new friends, and joining renga parties. He wrote in his journal, "I myself have been tempted for a long time by the cloud-moving wind—filled with a strong desire to wander." The above haiku is the last he wrote before he died at the age of 50.

Yosa Buson

**they end their flight
one by one
crows at dusk**

—Buson (1716-1784)

Taniguchi Buson was born in the village of Kerma (near Osaka, Japan) just 22 years after Basho's death. He left his wealthy family behind when he was 20 to travel and study the arts. It was then that he changed his first name from Taniguchi to Yosa. Although Buson published many poetry books in his lifetime, he was known mainly as a painter. In 1772, when he was 56 years old, his fame as a poet began to rise, but it wasn't until after his death, when Japanese poet Masako Shiki wrote about Buson's poetry in his essays, that he became widely known.

Kobayashi Issa

brilliant moon
is it true that you too
must pass in a hurry?

—Issa (1763-1828)

Issa (e-sah) was born, Kobayashi Nobuyuki in central Japan in 1763. His grandmother raised him after his mother died when he was a toddler. Issa was known to have compassion for the smallest of creatures. He often wrote about flies, fleas, and crickets with empathy, seeming to understand their feelings. When he was 30, he embarked on a ten-year trek through southwestern Japan. During this trip, he took the pen name Issa, which means "a cup of tea." He wrote 20,000 haiku in his lifetime. Issa didn't follow Basho or Buson's style of poetry. His subjects and style were unique; perhaps this is why he is still one of the most-loved haiku poets.

Masaoka Shiki

**consider me
as one who loved poetry
and persimmons**

—Shiki (1867-1902)

Shiki was born in 1867 into a samurai family with poetry in his soul. He contracted tuberculosis (a disease that affects the lungs) when he was 22 years old. After enlisting in the Japanese army, his illness became worse. Nevertheless, he continued to write poetry for all his 34 years of life and became well known in the literary world. Shiki brought current ideas to centuries-old rules of poetry. He believed poets should write about things as they are now and use everyday vocabulary. He defined the stand-alone haiku from the hokku (starting verse of a renga) as its own form and argued that it should be considered an official form of Japanese literature.

**I am going out
be good and play together
my cricket children**

—Kobayashi Issa

ABOUT THE AUTHOR

Danna (Dan-ah) Smith is a poet and award-winning author of over twenty-five books for children, including *Peek-A-Boo Haiku,* a lift-the-flap board book published by Simon & Schuster.

When she was young, a pen was Danna's favorite toy. She grew up weaving words into silly poems or stories that sparked emotion. She wrote her first poem when she was eight years old.

Born and raised in Salt Lake City, Utah, she was exposed to many creatures through her father, who trained, bred, and rehabilitated animals. It was common to find bobcats, alligators, monkeys, hawks, or even vultures at her home. A love of animals and nature has spilled into her love of writing. Today, her favorite toy is a computer keyboard.

Danna lives and creates in the beautiful northern California wine country. You can learn more about her and her books at www.dannasmithbooks.com or by scanning the Q.R. code below.

Haiku Dictionary

ginko (geen-ko): a walk outside to observe nature and write haiku.

gunsaku (goo'n-sah-coo): a collection of individual poems composed around the same subject written from different points of view.

haibun (hi-boon): a short story accompanied by a haiku. Popularized by Matsuo Basho in his travel journals.

haiga (hi-gah): a haiku with a sketch or painting.

haiku: (hi-coo) A short, three-line poem that focuses on nature and is written in simple language.

hokku (hoe'k-coo): the starting verse of renga (linked poem).

kigo (key-go): a seasonal word. Nouns which imply the season or time of year.

kireji (key-ray-jee): a cutting word. Japanese words used to create a break or pause. In English, punctuation like commas, exclamation points, dashes, and colons are used to achieve a pause.

kuhi (coo-hee): The Japanese word for carving a poem on a stone. Poem stones are seen in gardens, temples, and parks all over the world.

renga (Ray'n-gah): a linked poem of up to 100 verses written by a group of people, each verse having two or three lines.

rensaku (ray'n-sah-coo): A collection of haiku written on one subject that tells a complete story.

sabaki (sah-bah-key):a group coach or leader when writing renga. The English translation of the Japanese word sabaki is "judgement."

saijiki (sah-ee-jee-key): a book of seasonal words (kigo) used as a guide in the selection of nature words when writing haiku.

senryu (sen-you-rue): haiku's cousin. Named after the Japanese poet who first used the form. A brief poem where the focus is on human nature and people rather than nature, as in a haiku.

Recommended Reading

A Haiku Library

Enjoy these books featuring haiku. The recommended age is merely a suggestion. Haiku lovers of all ages will enjoy them:

Smith, Danna. **Peek-A-Boo Haiku**. Simon and Schuster, 21 Feb. 2023. (Preschool-grade 2) **This poetic lift-the-flap board book for young features haiku about hidden woodland animals, plus flaps that reveal those animals!**

Krina Patel-Sage. **Watch Me Bloom**. Lantana Publishing, 7 Mar. 2023. (Preschool-3) **Mindful haiku poems to help us rediscover our natural surroundings without traveling too far from home.**

Walker, Sally and McKay, Angela. **Trees: Haiku from Roots to Leaves**. Candlewick Press, 14 Mar 2023. (7-9**). In a unique melding of science and poetry, a collection of haiku extols the wonder of trees—and explores their vital roles on our living planet.**

Rosenberg, Sydell, and Amy Losak. **Wings Strokes Haiku**. 27 July. 2022 . **A well-rounded collection of haiku written by a mother and daughter team.**

Gianferrari, Maria. **Whoo-Ku Haiku: A Great Horned Owl Story**. Penguin, 3 Mar. 2020 (4-8) **Haiku leads young readers through the dramatic life cycle of one of America's most beloved wild animals.**

Sydell Rosenberg, and Sawsan Chalabi. **H Is for Haiku: A Treasury of Haiku from A to Z**. (5-11) Oklahoma City, Okay, Penny Candy Books, 2018. **In the collection of ABC Haiku, readers will learn how to notice small moments in city life**.

Ramirez-Christensen, Esperanza. **My First Book of Haiku Poems**. (K-4) Tuttle Publishing, 26 Mar. 2019. **Includes the original versions of the Japanese poems alongside the English translation to form a complete cultural experience**.

Laura Purdie Salas, and Mercè López. **Lion of the Sky: Haiku for All Seasons**.(5-9) Minneapolis, Millbrook Press, 2019. **Haiku meet riddles in this wonderful collection**.

Wardlaw, Lee. **Won Ton: A Cat Tale Told in Haiku**. (4-8) Henry Holt and Company (BYR), 15 Feb. 2011. **Written from the cat's perspective, this poetic book tells a story about a cat who is adopted by a little boy**.

Raczka, Bob. **Guyku: A Year of Haiku for Boys**. (4-7) Houghton Mifflin Harcourt, 4 Oct. 2010. **Boy-centric haiku about outdoor fun throughout the seasons**, with illustrations by the New York Times bestselling creator Peter Reynolds

Mannis, Celeste. **One Leaf Rides the Wind**.(5-8) National Geographic Books, 17 Mar. 2005. **This counting book takes kids through a Japanese garden and all there is to discover**.

Acknowledgments

First, I am grateful to the men and women who wrote haiku long ago and to the poets who continue to lead new generations in finding beauty in the world through words.

Much gratitude to the authors and poets who contributed their poetry in the making of this book: Kate Coombs, author of *Today I Am a River* (Sounds True), Nancy Etchemendy, author of *The Power of Un* (Scholastic), Matt Forrest Esenwine, author of *The Thing to Remember about Stargazing* (Tilbury House), Raven Howell, author of *Seasons* (Jan-Carol Pub), Linda Hoffman Kimball, author of *Come with Me on Halloween* (Albert Whitman Co), Amy Losak and Sydell Rosenberg, authors of *H is for Haiku* (Penny Candy Books) and *Wing Strokes Haiku,* (Kelsay Books), Bobi Martin, author of *Organisms that Glow* (Britannica), Poet, Angie Quantrell, Lee Wardlaw, author of *Won Ton: A Cat Tale Told in Haiku,* (Henry Holt), and Linda Whalen, author of *Little Red Rolls Away (Sleeping Bear Press)*— your words inspire!

To all those who encouraged, supported, and believed in me, I thank you.

And finally, to my husband and children, whom I love wholeheartedly. You are the frogs in my pond.

Permissions and Sources

"while a cicada..." Kobayashi Issa, loose translation/interpretation by Michael R. Burch.

"a warbler poops..." Uejima Onitsura Japanese poet, 1661-1738

"under cherry trees..." Matsuo Bashow, translated by Peter Beilenson, *Japanese Haiku* pg. 23.

Images:

Interior line art printed with permission under Canva Pro Content License, One Design.

Image Issa: Yoshi Canopus, CC BY-SA 3.0 via Wikimedia Commons.

Painting Basho: Hokusai, via Wikimedia Commons.

Image Buson: via Wikimedia Commons.

Portrait Masaoka Shiki: from Japanese book "Soseki no Omoide "via Wikimedia Commons.

Paint Blot Haiga: Poetry Pop, Poetry Pop Poetry Blog. July 7, 2023.
https://www.poetrypop.com.

Websites:

www.hsa-Haiku.org. Accessed July 8, 2023. https://www.hsa-haiku.org/index.htm.

Jack. 2017. "Haiku: A Whole Lot More than 5-7-5." Tofugu. October 10, 2017.
https://www.tofugu.com/japan/haiku/. Accessed May 2023

"The Haiku Foundation." n.d. The Haiku Foundation. https://thehaikufoundation.org/. Accessed
March 2023

Japanese poetry terms and American phonetic spellings compiled by Jane Reichhold via
aha.poetry.com and Haiku Society of American.com.

"Poetry Pop Poetry Blog." 2023. Poetry Pop Poetry Blog. July 7, 2023.
https://www.poetrypop.com.

Margolis, Eric. 2022. "There's More Going on in a Haiku than Just the 5-7-5 Syllable Rule." The
Japan Times. December 30, 2022.
https://www.japantimes.co.jp/life/2022/12/30/language/understanding-haiku/.

Books:

Goldberg, Natalie. 2021. Three Simple Lines: A Writer's Pilgrimage into the Heart and Homeland
of Haiku. Novato, California: New World Library.

Hass, Robert, Bashō Matsuo, Buson Yosa, and Issa Kobayashi. 1994. The Essential Haiku:
Versions of Bashō, Buson, and Issa. Hopewell, N.J.: Ecco Press. pg. 153,145

Higginson, William J, and Penny Harter. 2013.*Haiku Handbook*: How to Write, Teach, and
Appreciate Haiku.

Sato, Hiroaki. 1995.*One Hundred Frogs*, Shambhala Publications. The Early History of Renga pg.
41,

Yoshino, Yoshiko, "Budding Sakura," The Haiku Foundation Digital Library, accessed July 11,
2023, https://www.thehaikufoundation.org/omeka/items/show/1869.

Rosenstock, Gabriel. 2011.*Haiku Enlightenment*. Newcastle Upon Tyne: Cambridge Scholars Pub.

Japanese Haiku: 1955. Translated from the Masters of the Seventeen-Syllable Poetic Form, Basho, Buson and Others. [with Illustrations.].Peter Pauper Press 1955, Mount Vernon, N.Y.

Select Sources and Quotes:

"he (Issa) wrote 20,000 haiku... "Graceguts - for the Love of Issa." n.d. Www.graceguts.com. Accessed July 14, 2023. https://www.graceguts.com/essays/for-the-love-of-issa.

"time after time new sights..." *Basho the Complete Haiku* by Jane Reichhold Kodansha International pg. 70-71.

"sold his home outside Edo" *The Narrow Road to the Deep North* essay Britannica pg. 1.

"learn about the pine..." quoted in *The Essential Haiku*, Hass, Robert, pg. 233.

"Don't follow in the footsteps..." quoted in *The Essential Haiku*, Hass, Robert, pg. 233.

"is there any good..." quoted, poetryfoundation.org.

"if you write five haiku..." quoted in *Three Simple Lines*, Goldberg, Natalie, New World Library, pg. 6.

"ya" cutting words, The Japan Times, Dec 30, 2022, accessed May 2023

"Falling sick on my journey..." Tofugu. October 10, 2017. https://www.tofugu.com/japan/haiku/. accessed June 2023

"I myself have been tempted..." Basho journal, *Narrow Road to the Deep North*, translated by Nobuyuki Yuasa

Made in the USA
Monee, IL
12 May 2025

17278409R00059